A THOUGHT A DAY

Bible Wisdom

A BIBLE VERSE FOR EACH DAY

COMPILED BY BROOKE WEXLER

A THOUGHT A DAY

Bible Wisdom

A BIBLE VERSE FOR EACH DAY

COMPILED BY BROOKE WEXLER

All Scripture quotations are taken from the following sources: King James Version (KJV), Public Domain. The New King James Version® (NKJV®). Copyright © 1982 by Thomas Nelson, Inc. Used by permission. All rights reserved. The Holy Bible, New International Version® (NIV®). Copyright © 1973, 1978, 1984, 2011 by Biblica, Inc. All rights reserved worldwide. Used by permission. The Holy Bible, English Standard Version® (ESV®) Copyright © 2001 by Crossway, a publishing ministry of Good News Publishers. All rights reserved.

In the following Scripture quotations, the form L%#$ represents the Hebrew *Yahweh*, while *Lord* represents *Adonai*, in accordance with the Bible version used.

Compiled by Brooke Wexler
Design by Tseng Yu-Ting
ISBN: 978-1-63264-002-4

www.cascade-publishing.com
© 2023 Cascade Publishing, USA.
All Rights Reserved. Printed in China.

Galovac waterfall, Plitvice Lakes National Park, Croatia

Whom have I in heaven but thee? And there is none upon earth that I desire beside thee. ... God is the strength of my heart.

—Psalm 73:25–26 KJV

A wise man will hear and increase learning, and a man of understanding will attain wise counsel.

—Proverbs 1:5 NKJV

Eiffel Tower, Paris, France

January 3

Panyee Island, Thailand

Man shall not live by bread alone, but by every word that comes from the mouth of God.

—Matthew 4:4 ESV

January 4

Don Quixote and Sancho Panza statue on the Plaza de Espana, Madrid, Spain

In the gospel the righteousness of God is revealed—a righteousness that is by faith.

—Romans 1:17 NIV

January 5

Réunion Island, Overseas Department of Réunion, France

Blessed are those whose strength is in you. They go from strength to strength.

—Psalm 84:5, 7 ESV

January 6

The fear of the Lord is the beginning of knowledge, but fools despise wisdom and instruction.

—Proverbs 1:7 NKJV

Swallow's Nest, Crimea

January 7

North American Cougar, Jasper National Park, Alberta, Canada

You shall worship the Lord your God and him only shall you serve.

—Matthew 4:10 ESV

January 8

God "will repay each person according to what they have done."

—Romans 2:6 NIV

📍 Torch Bearer Statue at Gellert Hill, Budapest, Hungary

January 9

Ice caves at Rifle Mountain Park, Colorado, USA

Your words have upheld him who was stumbling, and you have made firm the feeble knees.

—Job 4:4 ESV

January 10

If you call out for insight and raise your voice for understanding, if you seek it like silver and search for it as for hidden treasures, then you will understand the fear of the LORD and find the knowledge of God.

—Proverbs 2:3–5 ESV

Old Town Colmar, France

Blessed are the poor in spirit, for theirs is the kingdom of heaven. Blessed are those who mourn, for they shall be comforted. Blessed are the meek, for they shall inherit the earth.

—Matthew 5:3–5 ESV

Skalnaté Lake, Tatra National Park, Slovakia

January 12

God does not show favoritism.

—Romans 2:11 NIV

Frederiksborg castle, Hillerød, Denmark

January 13

Is not your fear of God your confidence, and the integrity of your ways your hope?

—Job 4:6 ESV

Glen Canyon National Recreation Area, Utah, USA

January 14

Palace of Fine Arts, San Francisco, USA

The LORD gives wisdom; from his mouth come knowledge and understanding.

—Proverbs 2:6 NKJV

January 15

📍 Lake Huron, Port Hope, Michigan, USA

Blessed are those who hunger and thirst for righteousness, for they shall be satisfied.

—Matthew 5:6 ESV

January 16

Terracotta Warriors, Xi'an, China

Let God be true though every one were a liar.

—Romans 3:4 ESV

January 17

Skradinski falls, Krka National Park, Croatia

My prayer is to you, O LORD. At an acceptable time, O God, in the abundance of your steadfast love answer me in your saving faithfulness.

—Psalm 69:13 ESV

When wisdom enters your heart, and knowledge is pleasant to your soul, discretion will preserve you; understanding will keep you.

—Proverbs 2:10–11 NKJV

January 18

Piazza San Marco, Venice, Italy

January 19

📍 Alpine ibex, Chamonix Mont Blanc, France

Blessed are the merciful, for they shall receive mercy. Blessed are the pure in heart, for they shall see God. Blessed are the peacemakers, for they shall be called sons of God.

—Matthew 5:7–9 ESV

January 20

📍 The Men at Sea, Esbjerg harbor, Denmark

All have sinned and fall short of the glory of God, and all are justified freely by his grace through the redemption that came by Christ Jesus.

—Romans 3:23–24 NIV

January 21

Yu Long river and karst peaks, Yanshuo, Guangxi, China

To God would I commit my cause … he gives rain on the earth and sends waters on the fields; he sets on high those who are lowly, and those who mourn are lifted to safety.

—Job 5:8,10–11 ESV

January 22

Torii Gate, Miyajima, Japan

Let not mercy and truth forsake you; bind them around your neck, write them on the tablet of your heart.

—Proverbs 3:3 NKJV

January 23

Blessed are those who are persecuted for righteousness' sake, for theirs is the kingdom of heaven. Rejoice and be glad, for your reward is great in heaven.

—Matthew 5:10,12 ESV

Death Valley National Park, California, USA

January 24

📍 Friendship of the Peoples Fountain, Moscow, Russia

[Abraham] did not waver through unbelief … but was strengthened in his faith and gave glory to God, being fully persuaded that God had power to do what he had promised.

—Romans 4:20–21 NIV

January 25

📍 Arches National Park, Utah, USA

Teach me, and I will be silent; make me understand how I have gone astray.

—Job 6:24 ESV

January 26

📍 Belvedere Castle in Central Park, Manhattan, New York, USA

Trust in the Lord with all your heart, and lean not on your own understanding; in all your ways acknowledge Him, and He shall direct your paths.

—Proverbs 3:5–6 NKJV

January 27

📍 Andean mountain cat, Mount Piltriquitrón, Argentina

You are the light of the world. Let your light shine before others, so that they may see your good works and give glory to your Father who is in heaven.

—Matthew 5:14,16 ESV

January 28

📍 Basilica of Saint Mary of the Flower, Florence, Italy

We have peace with God through our Lord Jesus Christ.

—Romans 5:1 NIV

January 29

📍 Carpathian Mountains, Ukraine

How forceful are upright words!

—Job 6:25 ESV

January 30

Chalbi Desert, Kenya

Do not be wise in your own eyes; fear the Lord and depart from evil.

—Proverbs 3:7 NKJV

January 31

Reticulated giraffe, Samburu National Reserve, Kenya

Give to the one who begs from you, and do not refuse the one who would borrow from you.

—Matthew 5:42 ESV

February 1

We also glory in our sufferings, because we know that suffering produces perseverance; perseverance, character; and character, hope.

—Romans 5:3–4 NIV

📍 Christ of the Abyss underwater statue, Key Largo, Florida, USA

February 2

📍 Natural thermal hot springs, Salar, Bolivia

What is man, that you make so much of him, and that you set your heart on him, visit him every morning and test him every moment?

—Job 7:17–18 ESV

February 3

Katsura Imperial Gardens, Kyoto, Japan

Honor the Lord with your possessions … so your barns will be filled with plenty, and your vats will overflow with new wine.

—Proverbs 3:9–10 NKJV

February 4

Love your enemies and pray for those who persecute you, so that you may be sons of your Father who is in heaven. For he makes his sun rise on the evil and on the good, and sends rain on the just and on the unjust.

—Matthew 5:44–45 ESV

📍 Crested Blue Jay, Indiana, USA

February 5

God demonstrates his own love for us in this: While we were still sinners, Christ died for us.

—Romans 5:8 NIV

📍 The Clock of Citizens, Brussels, Belgium

February 6

Hunts Mesa, Monument Valley, Arizona, USA

You have granted me life and steadfast love, and your care has preserved my spirit.

—Job 10:12 ESV

February 7

📍 Igloo City, Cantwell, Alaska, USA

Happy is the man who finds wisdom … for her proceeds are better than the profits of silver, and her gain than fine gold. Her ways are ways of pleasantness, and all her paths are peace.

—Proverbs 3:13–14,17 NKJV

February 8

📍 Texel lambs, Friesland, The Netherlands

Beware of practicing your righteousness before other people in order to be seen by them, for then you will have no reward from your Father who is in heaven.

—Matthew 6:1 ESV

February 9

Although I want to do good, evil is right there with me. Thanks be to God, who delivers me through Jesus Christ our Lord!

—Romans 7:21,25 NIV

Angel of the North, Gateshead, Tyne and Wear, England

February 10

Segara Anak crater lake, Mount Rinjani, Lombok, Indonesia

Oh, that God would speak and open his lips to you, and that he would tell you the secrets of wisdom! For he is manifold in understanding.

—Job 11:5–6 ESV

February 11

📍 St. Vitus Cathedral, Prague, Czech Republic

Do not be afraid of sudden terror, nor of trouble from the wicked when it comes; for the Lord will be your confidence, and will keep your foot from being caught.

—Proverbs 3:25–26 NKJV

February 12

📍 Bohemian Switzerland National Park, Czech Republic

When you pray, go into your room and shut the door and pray to your Father who is in secret. And your Father who sees in secret will reward you.

—Matthew 6:6 ESV

February 13

There is now no condemnation for those who are in Christ Jesus.

—Romans 8:1 NIV

📍 Venus Salon ceiling, Castle of Versailles, France

February 14

Can you find out the deep things of God? Can you find out the limit of the Almighty? It is higher than heaven—what can you do? Deeper than Sheol—what can you know? Its measure is longer than the earth and broader than the sea.

—Job 11:7–9 ESV

📍 Aurora Borealis, Norway

February 15

Manzanares el Real Castle, Spain

Do not withhold good from those to whom it is due, when it is in the power of your hand to do so.

—Proverbs 3:27 NKJV

February 16

Our Father in heaven, hallowed be your name. Your kingdom come, your will be done. ... Give us this day our daily bread, and forgive us our debts, as we also have forgiven our debtors. And lead us not into temptation, but deliver us from evil.

—Matthew 6:9–13 ESV

Dutch bulbfields, South Holland, The Netherlands

Those who live according to the flesh have their minds set on what the flesh desires; but those who live in accordance with the Spirit have their minds set on what the Spirit desires.

—Romans 8:5 NIV

February 17

📍 Goldenes Dachl, Innsbruck, Austria

February 18

 Port Campbell National Park, Great Ocean Road, Victoria, Australia

Wisdom is with the aged, and understanding in length of days.

—Job 12:12 ESV

February 19

Bramante Staircase, Vatican Museum, Vatican City

Do not contend with a man for no reason, when he has done you no harm.

—Proverbs 3:30 ESV

February 20

📍 Elephant seal, Big Sur, California, USA

If you forgive others their trespasses, your heavenly Father will also forgive you, but if you do not forgive others their trespasses, neither will your Father forgive your trespasses.

—Matthew 6:14–15 ESV

February 21

I consider that our present sufferings are not worth comparing with the glory that will be revealed in us.

—Romans 8:18 NIV

📍 Minin and Pozharsky monument, St. Basil's Cathedral, Moscow, Russia

February 22

Twelve Apostles, Great Ocean Road, Victoria, Australia

Oh that you would keep silent, and it would be your wisdom!

—Job 13:5 ESV

February 23

The wise shall inherit glory, but shame shall be the legacy of fools.

—Proverbs 3:35 NKJV

Bratislava Castle, Bratislava, Slovakia

February 24

Nyalas antelope, Kruger National Park, South Africa

Look at the birds of the air: they neither sow nor reap nor gather into barns, and yet your heavenly Father feeds them. Are you not of more value than they?

—Matthew 6:26 ESV

February 25

Hope that is seen is no hope at all. Who hopes for what they already have? But if we hope for what we do not yet have, we wait for it patiently.

—Romans 8:24–25 NIV

📍 Monument to the Immigrant, New Orleans, Louisiana, USA

February 26

I know that my Redeemer lives.

—Job 19:25 ESV

📍 Caucasus Mountains, Georgia

February 27

📍 Brooklyn Bridge, New York, USA

Get wisdom, get understanding. ... Forsake her not, and she shall preserve thee: love her, and she shall keep thee.

—Proverbs 4:5–6 KJV

February 28

Tulip fields, Groningen, The Netherlands

Seek first the kingdom of God and his righteousness, and all these things will be added to you.

—Matthew 6:33 ESV

February 29

We know that in all things God works for the good of those who love him, who have been called according to his purpose.

—Romans 8:28 NIV

📍 Turkish lanterns, Grand Bazaar, Istanbul, Turkey

March 1

Beihai Tunnel, Matsu Island, Taiwan

Agree with God, and be at peace; thereby good will come to you. Receive instruction from his mouth, and lay up his words in your heart.

—Job 22:21–22 ESV

March 2

Liberty Square, Taipei, Taiwan

Wisdom is the principal thing; therefore get wisdom. ... Exalt her, and she will promote you; she will bring you honor.

—Proverbs 4:7–8 NKJV

March 3

📍 The Swiss Alps

Do not be anxious about tomorrow. … Sufficient for the day is its own trouble.

—Matthew 6:34 ESV

March 4

I am convinced that neither death nor life, neither angels nor demons, neither the present nor the future, nor any powers, neither height nor depth, nor anything else in all creation, will be able to separate us from the love of God.

—Romans 8:38–39 NIV

Place de la Concorde, Paris, France

March 5

⚲ Goðafoss Waterfall, Iceland

[God] knows the way that I take; when he has tried me, I shall come out as gold.

—Job 23:10 ESV

March 6

Facade of the ancient Celsus Library, Ephesus, Turkey

The path of the just is as the shining light, that shineth more and more unto the perfect day.

—Proverbs 4:18 KJV

March 7

📍 Lake Tahoe, Serra Nevada mountain range, Between California and Nevada, USA

Judge not, that you be not judged.

—Matthew 7:1 ESV

March 8

Everyone who calls on the name of the Lord will be saved.

—Romans 10:13 NIV

◉ Thracian Tomb of Kazanlak, Kazanlak, Bulgaria

March 9

Village path, Swiss Alps, Switzerland

He is unchangeable, and who can turn him back? What he desires, that he does. For he will complete what he appoints for me.

—Job 23:13–14 ESV

March 10

📍 Doonagore Castle, County Clare, Ireland

Keep your heart with all diligence, for out of it spring the issues of life.

—Proverbs 4:23 NKJV

March 11

📍 Berjaya rainforest, Langkawi, Malaysia

Ask, and it will be given to you; seek, and you will find; knock, and it will be opened to you.

—Matthew 7:7 ESV

March 12

📍 Oil paper umbrellas, Meinong, Kaohsiung, Taiwan

God's gifts and his call are irrevocable.

—Romans 11:29 NIV

March 13

Crimean Mountains

The Spirit of God has made me, and the breath of the Almighty gives me life.

—Job 33:4 ESV

March 14

Chain bridge, Budapest, Hungary

Wisdom is better than rubies, and all the things one may desire cannot be compared with her.

—Proverbs 8:11 NKJV

March 15

Whatever you wish that others would do to you, do also to them.

—Matthew 7:12 ESV

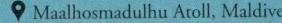
Maalhosmadulhu Atoll, Maldives

March 16

Oh, the depth of the riches of the wisdom and knowledge of God! How unsearchable his judgments, and his paths beyond tracing out! "Who has known the mind of the Lord? Or who has been his counselor?"

—Romans 11:33–34 NIV

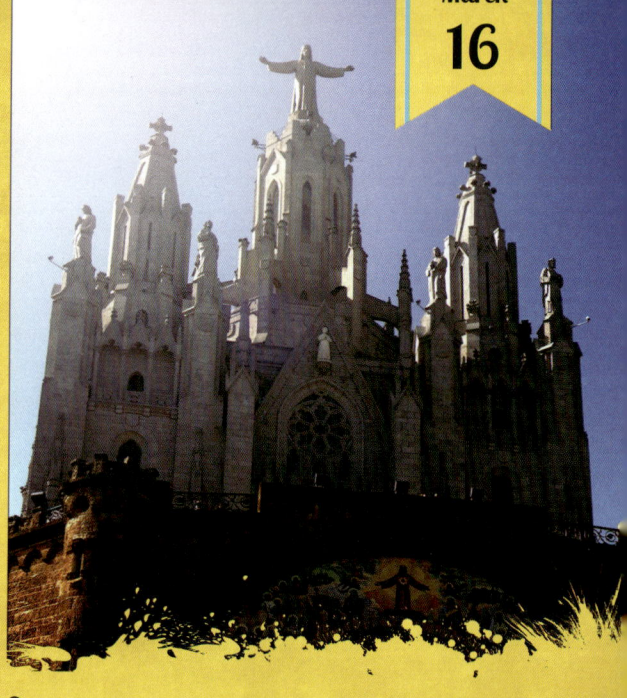

Expiatory Church of the Sacred Heart of Jesus, Barcelona, Spain

March 17

Halong Bay, Quang Ninh Province, Vietnam

God is mighty, and does not despise any; he is mighty in strength of understanding.

—Job 36:5 ESV

March 18

Ancient Bagan City, Mandalay Region, Myanmar

Give instruction to a wise man, and he will be yet wiser: teach a just man, and he will increase in learning.

—Proverbs 9:9 KJV

March 19

Great tit, New Forest National Park, England

Those who are well have no need of a physician, but those who are sick. ... I came not to call the righteous, but sinners.

—Matthew 9:12–13 ESV

March 20

Cibeles Fountain, Madrid, Spain

I know that you can do all things, and that no purpose of yours can be thwarted.

—Job 42:2 ESV

March 21

Haleakala Crater, Maui, Hawaii, USA

The fear of the Lord is the beginning of wisdom, and the knowledge of the Holy One is understanding.

—Proverbs 9:10 NKJV

March
22

According to your faith be it done to you.

—Matthew 9:29 ESV

◉ Neuschwanstein Castle, Bavaria, Germany

March 23

Rocky Mountain goats, La Plata Peak, Ellingwood Ridge, Rocky Mountains, Colorado, USA

Do not conform to the pattern of this world, but be transformed by the renewing of your mind. Then you will be able to test and approve what God's will is.

—Romans 12:2 NIV

Blessed is the man who walks not in the counsel of the wicked ... but his delight is in the law of the LORD. ... He is like a tree planted by streams of water that yields its fruit in its season. ... In all that he does, he prospers.

—Psalm 1:1–3 ESV

March 24

Statue of Imre Nagy, Budapest, Hungary

March 25

📍 Rioni River, Caucasus Mountains, Georgia

Treasures of wickedness profit nothing, but righteousness delivers from death. The Lord will not allow the righteous soul to famish.

—Proverbs 10:2–3 NKJV

March 26

When he saw the crowds, he had compassion for them, because they were … like sheep without a shepherd. Then he said … "The harvest is plentiful, but the laborers are few; therefore pray earnestly to the Lord of the harvest to send out laborers into his harvest."

—Matthew 9:36–38 ESV

Luxembourg City, Luxembourg

March 27

Southern ostrich, Tsitsikamma National Park, Garden Route, South Africa

Do not think of yourself more highly than you ought, but rather think of yourself with sober judgment.

—Romans 12:3 NIV

March 28

Answer me when I call, O God! … You have given me relief when I was in distress. Be gracious to me and hear my prayer!

—Psalm 4:1 ESV

📍 Virginia Washington Monument, Richmond, Virginia, USA

March 29

Sol de Mañana, Bolivia

He who has a slack hand becomes poor, but the hand of the diligent makes rich.

—Proverbs 10:4 NKJV

March 30

📍 Oia, Santorini Island, Greece

I am sending you out as sheep in the midst of wolves, so be wise as serpents and innocent as doves.

—Matthew 10:16 ESV

📍 Lake Vanajavesi, Aulanko National Park, Finland

Be joyful in hope, patient in affliction, faithful in prayer. Share with the Lord's people who are in need. Practice hospitality.

—Romans 12:12–13 NIV

April 1

📍 Arch of Constantine, Rome, Italy

I will both lay me down in peace, and sleep: for thou, Lord, only makest me dwell in safety.

—Psalm 4:8 KJV

April 2

Svartifoss (Black Waterfall), Iceland

The memory of the righteous is blessed.

—Proverbs 10:7 NKJV

April 3

Charles Bridge over the Vltava River, Prague, Czech Republic

Nothing is covered that will not be revealed, or hidden that will not be known.

—Matthew 10:26 ESV

Live in harmony with one another. Do not be proud, but be willing to associate with people of low position. Do not be conceited.

—Romans 12:16 NIV

April 4

Hawaiian Spinner Dolphin, Hawaii, USA

Lead me, O LORD,
in your righteousness
... make your way
straight before me.

—Psalm 5:8 ESV

April 5

📍 Iskor glazed ceramics, Rishton, Uzbekistan

Gomantong Caves, Borneo island, Malaysia

Hatred stirs up strife, but love covers all sins.

—Proverbs 10:12 NKJV

Come to me, all who labor and are heavy laden, and I will give you rest. Take my yoke upon you, and learn from me, for I am gentle and lowly in heart, and you will find rest for your souls. For my yoke is easy, and my burden is light.

—Matthew 11:28–30 ESV

April 7

Gadisar Lake, Jaisalmer, Rajasthan, India

April 8

Lesser and Greater Flamingos, Lake Nakuru, Kenya

Do not repay anyone evil for evil. … Live at peace with everyone. Do not take revenge. … Do not be overcome by evil, but overcome evil with good.

—Romans 12:17–19,21 NIV

April 9

Let all who take refuge in you rejoice; let them ever sing for joy. … For you bless the righteous, O LORD; you cover him with favor as with a shield.

—Psalm 5:11–12 ESV

📍 Statue of pope John-Paul II, Almudena Cathedral, Madrid, Spain

April 10

Heaven-Linking Avenue, Tianmen Mountain National Park, Zhangjiajie, Hunan Province, China

In the multitude of words sin is not lacking, but he who restrains his lips is wise.

—Proverbs 10:19 NKJV

April 11

📍 Caerlaverock Castle, Dumfries Shire, Scotland

On the day of judgment people will give account for every careless word they speak, for by your words you will be justified, and by your words you will be condemned.

—Matthew 12:36–37 ESV

April 12

Cherry trees in Sakura season, Japan

Give to everyone what you owe them: If you owe taxes, pay taxes; if revenue, then revenue; if respect, then respect; if honor, then honor.

—Romans 13:7 NIV

April 13

The LORD has heard the sound of my weeping. The LORD has heard my plea; the LORD accepts my prayer.

—Psalm 6:8–9 ESV

📍 Trinity Cathedral, Ipatiev Monastery, Kostroma, Russia

April 14

Meke crater lake, Konya, Turkey

The blessing of the Lord makes one rich, and He adds no sorrow with it.

—Proverbs 10:22 NKJV

April 15

📍 Basilica Cistern, Istanbul, Turkey

Whoever would be great among you must be your servant.

—Matthew 20:26 ESV

April 16

Caribou, Denali National Park, Alaska, USA

Each of us will give an account of ourselves to God. Therefore let us stop passing judgment on one another.

—Romans 14:12–13 NIV

April 17

What is man that you are mindful of him, and the son of man that you care for him? Yet you have made him a little lower than the heavenly beings and crowned him with glory and honor.

—Psalm 8:4–5 ESV

📍 Wies Church, Steingaden, Bavaria, Germany

April 18

When pride comes, then comes shame; but with the humble is wisdom.

—Proverbs 11:2 NKJV

Cliffs of Moher, County Clare, Ireland

April 19

Hohenzollern Castle, Baden-Württemberg, Germany

Whatever you ask in prayer, you will receive, if you have faith.

—Matthew 21:22 ESV

April 20

Japanese Maple, Japan

Let us therefore make every effort to do what leads to peace and to mutual edification.

—Romans 14:19 NIV

April 21

The Lord also will be a refuge for the oppressed, a refuge in times of trouble.

—Psalm 9:9 KJV

📍 Bear and Strawberry Tree statue, Madrid, Spain

April 22

📍 Eastern Alps, Austria

The integrity of the upright will guide them.

—Proverbs 11:3 NKJV

April 23

You shall love the Lord your God with all your heart and with all your soul and with all your mind. This is the great and first commandment. And a second is like it: You shall love your neighbor as yourself.

—Matthew 22:37–39 ESV

Tourlitis Lighthouse, Andros Island, Greece

April 24

📍 Sri Lankan Leopard, Yala National Park, Sri Lanka

We who are strong ought to bear with the failings of the weak.

—Romans 15:1 NIV

April 25

Those who know your name put their trust in you, for you, O LORD, have not forsaken those who seek you.

—Psalm 9:10 ESV

📍 Rathaus-Glockenspiel, Munich, Bavaria, Germany

April 26

Pasterze Glacier, Eastern Alps, Austria

A man of understanding holds his peace.

—Proverbs 11:12 NKJV

April 27

📍 Château de Versailles, France

Whoever exalts himself will be humbled, and whoever humbles himself will be exalted.

—Matthew 23:12 ESV

April 28

📍 Azure Window, Gozo island, Malta

Accept one another, then, just as Christ accepted you.

—Romans 15:7 NIV

April 29

📍 Hermitage of El Rocío, Andalusia, Spain

I have trusted in your steadfast love; my heart shall rejoice in your salvation.

—Psalm 13:5 ESV

April 30

Roussanou Monastery, Meteora, Greece

Where there is no counsel, the people fall; but in the multitude of counselors there is safety.

—Proverbs 11:14 NKJV

Crystal Palace, Retiro Park, Madrid, Spain

Truly, I say to you, as you did it to one of the least of these my brothers, you did it to me.

—Matthew 25:40 ESV

Chollas Cactus Garden, Joshua Tree National Park, California, USA

May the God of hope fill you with all joy and peace as you trust in him.

—Romans 15:13 NIV

May 3

I will sing to the LORD, because he has dealt bountifully with me.

—Psalm 13:6 ESV

📍 Vittorio Emanuele II gallery, Milan, Italy

May 4

Monterey Bay Sanctuary, California, USA

The generous soul will be made rich, and he who waters will also be watered himself.

—Proverbs 11:25 NKJV

May 5

Széchenyi Medicinal Bath, Budapest, Hungary

I am with you always, to the end of the age.

—Matthew 28:20 ESV

May 6

📍 Olympic National Park, Washington, USA

"What no eye has seen, what no ear has heard, and what no human mind has conceived"—the things God has prepared for those who love him.

—1 Corinthians 2:9 NIV

The lines have fallen for me in pleasant places; indeed, I have a beautiful inheritance.

—Psalm 16:6 ESV

May 7

Johann Strauss Monument, Stadtpark, Vienna, Austria

May 8

Grand Canyon National Park, Arizona, USA

The recompense of a man's hands will be rendered to him.

—Proverbs 12:14 NKJV

May 9

Colosseum, Rome, Italy

No one puts new wine into old wineskins. … New wine is for fresh wineskins.

—Mark 2:22 ESV

May 10

Tibetan Yak, Yamdrok lake, Xizang, China

What do you have that you did not receive? And if you did receive it, why do you boast as though you did not?

—1 Corinthians 4:7 NIV

📍 Inside Notre-Dame Basilica, Montreal, Canada

May 11

I bless the LORD who gives me counsel; in the night also my heart instructs me.

—Psalm 16:7 ESV

May 12

Grand Canyon of the Yellowstone, Yellowstone National Park, Wyoming, USA

The way of a fool is right in his own eyes, but he who heeds counsel is wise.

—Proverbs 12:15 NKJV

May 13

Lak lake, Daklak province, Vietnam

The Sabbath was made for man, not man for the Sabbath.

—Mark 2:27 ESV

Knowledge puffs up while love builds up.

—1 Corinthians 8:1 NIV

Tea plantation, Munnar, Kerala, India

May 15

I have set the Lord always before me ... I shall not be moved.

—Psalm 16:8 KJV

📍 Statue of St. Peter, St. Peter's Square and Basilica, Vatican City

May 16

Haew Narok Waterfall, Khao Yai National Park, Thailand

He who speaks truth declares righteousness.

—Proverbs 12:17 NKJV

If you ask me anything in my name, I will do it.

—John 14:14 ESV

May 17

Vernazza, La Spezia, Liguria, Italy

May 18

📍 Japanese Macaques, Jigokudani Monkey Park, Yamanouchi, Nagano Prefecture, Japan

Those who think they know something do not yet know as they ought to know.

—1 Corinthians 8:2 NIV

May 19

📍 San Cayetano Church, Madrid, Spain

You make known to me the path of life; in your presence there is fullness of joy; at your right hand are pleasures forevermore.

—Psalm 16:11 ESV

May 20

Vermilion Lakes, Banff National Park, Alberta, Canada

The hand of the diligent will rule.

—Proverbs 12:24 NKJV

May 21

📍 Djurdjevica Tara Bridge, Durmitor National Park, Montenegro

Is a lamp brought in to be put under a basket, or under a bed, and not on a stand?

—Mark 4:21 ESV

May 22

Nugget Point, Otago, New Zealand

Whatever you do, do it all for the glory of God.

—1 Corinthians 10:31 NIV

May 23

Hold up my goings in thy paths, that my footsteps slip not.

—Psalm 17:5 KJV

📍 Richard Coeur de Lion, Palace of Westminster, London, England

May 24

Olkhon Island Cave, Lake Baikal, Siberia, Russia

Heaviness in the heart of man maketh it stoop: but a good word maketh it glad.

—Proverbs 12:25 KJV

Cappadocia, Central Anatolia Region, Turkey

May 25

With the measure you use, it will be measured to you. … To the one who has, more will be given.

—Mark 4:24–25 ESV

May 26

There are different kinds of gifts, but the same Spirit distributes them. There are different kinds of service, but the same Lord. There are different kinds of working, but … it is the same God at work.

—1 Corinthians 12:4–6 NIV

Bolshoy Yugan River, Siberia, Russia

May 27

The Lord my God will enlighten my darkness.

—Psalm 18:28 KJV

Westerplatte Monument, Gdansk, Poland

May 28

Caucasus Mountains, Georgia

Hope deferred makes the heart sick, but when the desire comes, it is a tree of life.

—Proverbs 13:12 NKJV

May 29

Peace! Be still!

—Mark 4:39 ESV

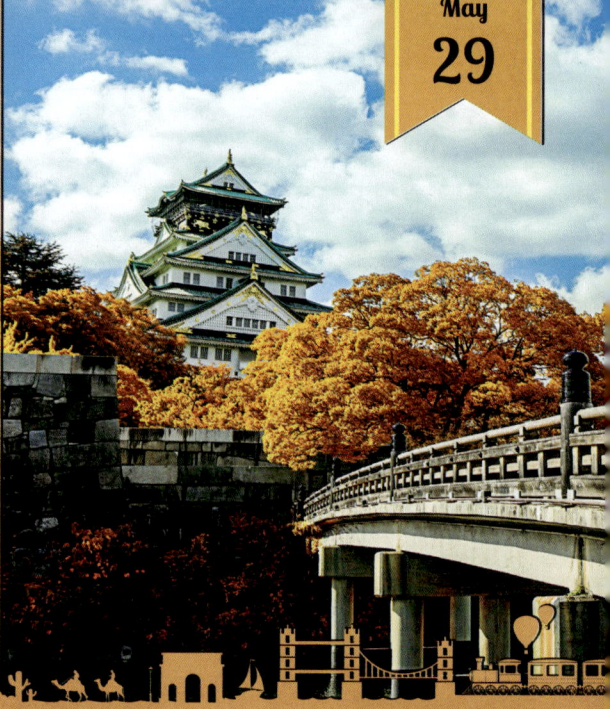

Osaka Castle, Osaka, Japan

May 30

Love is patient, love is kind. It does not envy, it does not boast, it is not proud. … It is not self-seeking, it is not easily angered, it keeps no record of wrongs. … It always protects, always trusts, always hopes, always perseveres. Love never fails.
—1 Corinthians 13:4, 5, 7, 8 NIV

Polar Bear mother and cubs, Canadian Arctic

May 31

Your gentleness made me great.

—Psalm 18:35 ESV

Lion of Saint Mark, Venice, Italy

📍 The French Alps, Rhône-Alpes region, France

He who is slow to wrath has great understanding, but he who is impulsive exalts folly.

—Proverbs 14:29 NKJV

June 2

Stowe Community Church, Stowe, Vermont, USA

Daughter, your faith has made you well; go in peace, and be healed of your disease.

—Mark 5:34 ESV

June 3

📍 Alaskan Brown Bear, Brooks Falls, Katmai National Park, Alaska, USA

Stand firm. Let nothing move you. Always give yourselves fully to the work of the Lord, because you know that your labor in the Lord is not in vain.

—1 Corinthians 15:58 NIV

The heavens declare the glory of God, and the sky above proclaims his handiwork.

—Psalm 19:1 ESV

June 4

📍 Corcovado mountain, Rio de Janeiro, Brazil

Roman-Kosh peak, Crimean Mountains

A sound heart is the life of the flesh: but envy the rottenness of the bones.

—Proverbs 14:30 KJV

June 6

Fenghuang ancient town, Hunan, China

Peace I leave with you; my peace I give to you. Let not your hearts be troubled, neither let them be afraid.

—John 14:27 ESV

June 7

Gray Kangaroo, Mackay, Queensland, Australia

Stand firm in the faith; be courageous; be strong. Do everything in love.

—1 Corinthians 16:13–14 NIV

June 8

The precepts of the LORD are right, rejoicing the heart; the commandment of the LORD is pure, enlightening the eyes.

—Psalm 19:8 ESV

○ Cathedral of Saint Lazarus, Autun, France

June 9

Railay Peninsula, Andaman coast, Thailand

A soft answer turns away wrath, but a harsh word stirs up anger.

—Proverbs 15:1 NKJV

Hungarian Parliament Building, Budapest, Hungary

June 10

Come away by yourselves to a desolate place and rest a while.

—Mark 6:31 ESV

June 11

Zhongsha Coral Reef, South China Sea

God … comforts us in all our troubles, so that we can comfort those in any trouble with the comfort we ourselves receive.

—2 Corinthians 1:3–4 NIV

June 12

📍 Russalka Memorial, Tallinn, Estonia

Let the words of my mouth, and the meditation of my heart, be acceptable in thy sight, O LORD, my strength, and my redeemer.

—Psalm 19:14 KJV

June 13

Bell Cave, Beit Guvrin national park, Israel

A wholesome tongue is a tree of life, but perverseness in it breaks the spirit.

—Proverbs 15:4 NKJV

June 14

Eilean Donan Castle, Kintail National Scenic Area, Scotland

Take heart; it is I. Do not be afraid.

—Mark 6:50 ESV

June 15

📍 Free-roaming Arabian horses, Queensland, Australia

We all, who ... contemplate the Lord's glory, are being transformed into his image.

—2 Corinthians 3:18 NIV

June 16

May [God] grant you your heart's desire and fulfill all your plans!

—Psalm 20:4 ESV

Melk Abbey Library, Melk, Austria

June 17

Ice Castles, Midway, Utah, USA

A merry heart maketh a cheerful countenance: but by sorrow of the heart the spirit is broken.

—Proverbs 15:13 KJV

June 18

📍 Hawa Mahal, Jaipur, Rajasthan, India

There is nothing outside a person that by going into him can defile him, but the things that come out of a person are what defile him. For from within … come evil thoughts.

—Mark 7:15–16,21 ESV

June 19

📍 Masca Valley, Tenerife, Canary Islands, Spain

We are hard pressed on every side, but not crushed; perplexed, but not in despair; persecuted, but not abandoned; struck down, but not destroyed.

—2 Corinthians 4:8, 9 NIV

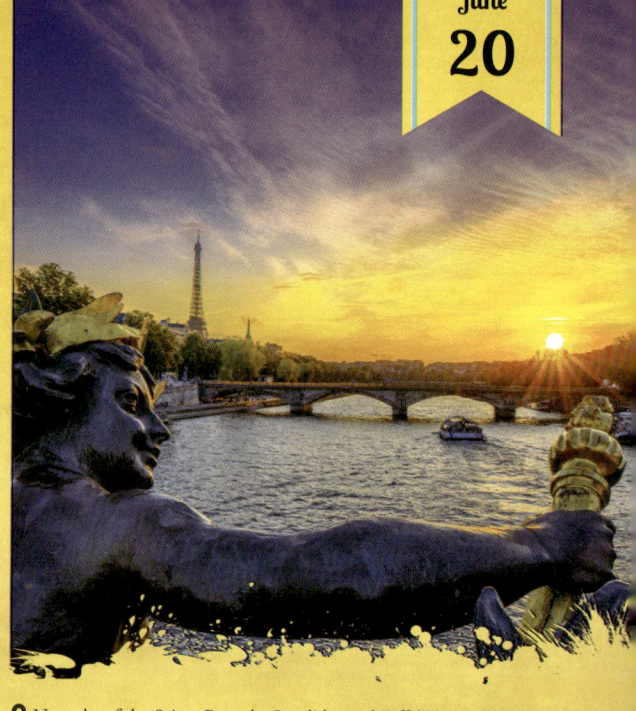

June 20

The LORD is my shepherd; I shall not want. He maketh me to lie down in green pastures: he leadeth me beside the still waters. He restoreth my soul: he leadeth me in the paths of righteousness.

—Psalm 23:1–3 KJV

Nymphs of the Seine, Pont des Invalides and Eiffel Tower, Paris, France

June 21

Isle of Skye, Inner Hebrides, Scotland

Better is a little with the fear of the Lord, than great treasure with trouble. Better is a dinner of herbs where love is, than a fatted calf with hatred.

—Proverbs 15:16–17 NKJV

June 22

📍 Kotikal Cave, Mamallapuram, Tamil Nadu, India

I have compassion on the crowd.

—Mark 8:2 ESV

June 23

Our light and momentary troubles are achieving for us an eternal glory that far outweighs them all. So we fix our eyes not on what is seen, but on what is unseen, since what is seen is temporary, but what is unseen is eternal.

—2 Corinthians 4:17–18 NIV

Caucasus mountains, Georgia

June 24

He who has clean hands and a pure heart, who does not lift up his soul to what is false and does not swear deceitfully. He will receive blessing from the LORD.

—Psalm 24:4–5 ESV

📍 "Angel with the Sponge" by Antonio Giorgetti, Ponte Sant'Angelo, Rome, Italy

June 25

Sajama National Park, Andean Plateau, Bolivia

Without counsel, plans go awry, but in the multitude of counselors they are established.

—Proverbs 15:22 NKJV

June 26

You are not setting your mind on the things of God, but on the things of man.

—Mark 8:33 ESV

Sigiriya rock fortress, Sri Lanka

June 27

📍 Jökulsárlón Lagoon, Iceland

If anyone is in Christ, the new creation has come: The old has gone, the new is here!

—2 Corinthians 5:17 NIV

June 28

The meek will he guide in judgment: and the meek will he teach his way. All the paths of the Lord are mercy and truth.

—Psalm 25:9–10 KJV

📍 Saint Isaac's Cathedral, Saint Petersburg, Russia

June 29

Seljalandsfoss waterfall, Iceland

A man has joy by the answer of his mouth, and a word spoken in due season, how good it is!

—Proverbs 15:23 NKJV

June 30

If anyone would come after me, let him deny himself and take up his cross and follow me. For whoever would save his life will lose it, but whoever loses his life for my sake and the gospel's will save it.

—Mark 8:34–35 ESV

Lotus Mahal, Vijayanagara ruins, Karnataka, India

July 1

Common House Sparrows (Passer domesticus)

I will be a Father to you, and you will be my sons and daughters, says the Lord Almighty.

—2 Corinthians 6:18 NIV

July 2

The Lord is my light and my salvation; whom shall I fear? The Lord is the strength of my life; of whom shall I be afraid?

—Psalm 27:1 KJV

Ceiling Fresco, Pilgrimage Church of Wies, Bavaria, Germany

July 3

Sol de Mañana, Bolivia

He who disdains instruction despises his own soul, but he who heeds rebuke gets understanding.

—Proverbs 15:32 NKJV

July 4

📍 Plaza del Cabildo, Seville, Spain

For what does it profit a man to gain the whole world and forfeit his soul? For what can a man give in return for his soul?

—Mark 8:36, 37 ESV

July 5

📍 European Wild Rabbit (Oryctolagus cuniculus)

God, who comforts the downcast, comforted us.

—2 Corinthians 7:6 NIV

July 6

📍 The Gallery of Maps, Belvedere Courtyard, Apostolic Palace, Vatican City

Teach me thy way, O LORD, and lead me in a plain path.

—Psalm 27:11 KJV

July 7

📍 Malá Fatra National Park, Slovakia

The fear of the Lord is the instruction of wisdom, and before honor is humility.

—Proverbs 15:33 NKJV

July 8

📍 Rijksmuseum, Amsterdam, Netherlands

All things are possible for one who believes.

—Mark 9:23 ESV

July 9

📍 Argentino Lake, Los Glaciares National Park, Santa Cruz Province, Argentina

Godly sorrow brings repentance that leads to salvation and leaves no regret, but worldly sorrow brings death.

—2 Corinthians 7:10 NIV

July 10

📍 Bethesda Terrace Arcade and Fountain, Central Park, New York, USA

Wait on the LORD: be of good courage, and he shall strengthen thine heart: wait, I say, on the LORD.

—Psalm 27:14 KJV

July 11

📍 Štrbské Pleso, High Tatras, Slovakia

Commit your works to the Lord, and your thoughts will be established.

—Proverbs 16:3 NKJV

July 12

If anyone would be first, he must be last of all and servant of all.

—Mark 9:35 ESV

Museumsinsel, Spree River, Berlin, Germany

July 13

📍 Salt deposits, Dead Sea, Jordan

Whoever sows sparingly will also reap sparingly, and whoever sows generously will also reap generously.

—2 Corinthians 9:6 NIV

July 14

📍 The Thinker, Rodin Museum, Paris, France

The LORD is my strength and my shield … therefore my heart greatly rejoiceth; and with my song will I praise him.

—Psalm 28:7 KJV

Better is a little with righteousness than great revenues without right.

—Proverbs 16:8 KJV

July 15

Olympus National Park, Greece

July 16

Corvin Castle, Hunedoara, Romania

Peace be with you.

—John 20:19

July 17

📍 Picture Lake and Mount Shuksan, Washington, USA

Each of you should give what you have decided in your heart to give, not reluctantly or under compulsion, for God loves a cheerful giver.

—2 Corinthians 9:7 NIV

July 18

📍 Ettal Abbey Dome Fresco, Ettal, Bavaria, Germany

The LORD will give strength unto his people; the LORD will bless his people with peace.

—Psalm 29:11 KJV

July 19

Danxia landform, Zhangye, Gansu, China

How much better to get wisdom than gold! And to get understanding is to be chosen rather than silver.

—Proverbs 16:16 NKJV

📍 Library of Celsus ruins, Ephesus, Turkey

Salt is good, but if the salt has lost its saltiness, how will you make it salty again? Have salt in yourselves, and be at peace with one another.

—Mark 9:50 ESV

July 21

God is able to bless you abundantly, so that in all things at all times, having all that you need, you will abound in every good work.

—2 Corinthians 9:8 NIV

📍 Saker Falcon

July 22

📍 Raíces Fountain, Paseo de la Princesa, Old San Juan, Puerto Rico

Weeping may endure for a night, but joy cometh in the morning.

—Psalm 30:5 KJV

July 23

Pride goes before destruction, and a haughty spirit before a fall.

—Proverbs 16:18 NKJV

📍 Eastern Coast, China

July 24

Forbidden City, Beijing, China

A man shall leave his father and mother and hold fast to his wife, and the two shall become one flesh.

—Mark 10:7–8 ESV

July 25

📍 Coniferous forest, Swiss Alps, Switzerland

[The Lord] said to me, "My grace is sufficient for you, for my power is made perfect in weakness." … For when I am weak, then I am strong.

—2 Corinthians 12:9–10 NIV

July 26

📍 Duomo di Milano, Piazza del Duomo, Milan, Lombardy, Italy

You have turned for me my mourning into dancing.

—Psalm 30:11 KJV

July 27

Better to be of a humble spirit with the lowly, than to divide the spoil with the proud.

—Proverbs 16:19 NKJV

📍 Sarika Waterfall, Khao Yai National Park, Thailand

July 28

📍 Matera, Basilicata, Italy

Let the children come to me; do not hinder them, for to such belongs the kingdom of God. ... Whoever does not receive the kingdom of God like a child shall not enter it.

—Mark 10:14–15 ESV

July 29

Northern lights, Lapland, Finland

A little yeast works through the whole batch of dough.

—Galatians 5:9 NIV

July 30

St Mary's Cathedral and Archibald Fountain in Hyde Park, Sydney, Australia

I will instruct you and teach you in the way you should go; I will counsel you with my eye upon you.

—Psalm 32:8 ESV

July 31

Tunnel of Love, Klevan, Ukraine

He that handleth a matter wisely shall find good: and whoso trusteth in the LORD, happy is he.

—Proverbs 16:20 KJV

Château de Sully-sur-Loire, France

All things are possible with God.

—Mark 10:27 ESV

August 2

Keukenhof gardens, Lisse, The Netherlands

The entire law is fulfilled in keeping this one command: "Love your neighbor as yourself."

—Galatians 5:14 NIV

August 3

📍 Ceiling Decoration, Palazzo Vecchio, Florence, Italy

The word of the Lord is upright, and all his work is done in faithfulness. He loves righteousness and justice; the earth is full of the steadfast love of the Lord.

—Psalm 33:4–5 ESV

August 4

Lava meets the sea, Volcanoes National Park, Big Island, Hawaii, USA

He who is slow to anger is better than the mighty, and he who rules his spirit than he who takes a city.

—Proverbs 16:32 NKJV

August 5

Tarkhankut Lighthouse, Crimea

Your faith has made you well.

—Mark 10:52 ESV

August 6

📍 Moon Jellyfish (Aurelia sp), Jellyfish Lake, Eil Malk Island, Palau

The fruit of the Spirit is love, joy, peace, forbearance, kindness, goodness, faithfulness, gentleness and self-control.

—Galatians 5:22–23 NIV

📍 Detail from The Creation of Adam, Genesis, Sistine Chapel, Apostolic Palace, Vatican City

Our soul waits for the Lord; he is our help and our shield. Let your steadfast love, O Lord, be upon us, even as we hope in you.

—Psalm 33:20,22 ESV

August 8

Cave Stream Scenic Reserve, Canterbury, New Zealand

The refining pot is for silver and the furnace for gold, but the Lord tests the hearts.

—Proverbs 17:3 NKJV

August 9

Puente Nuevo, Ronda, Andalusia, Spain

Have faith in God.

—Mark 11:22 ESV

August 10

📍 Anna's Hummingbird (Calypte anna)

Carry each other's burdens, and in this way you will fulfill the law of Christ.

—Galatians 6:2 NIV

Last Judgment fresco, Cathedral of Saint Mary of the Flower, Florence, Italy

Taste and see that the LORD is good: blessed is the man that trusteth in him.

—Psalm 34:8 KJV

August 12

📍 Braies Lake in the Dolomite Mountains, Sudtirol, Italy

Children's children are the crown of old men; and the glory of children are their fathers.

—Proverbs 17:6 KJV

August 13

Traditional stilt fishing, Galle, Sri Lanka

Whatever you ask in prayer, believe that you have received it, and it will be yours.

—Mark 11:24 ESV

August 14

Bactrian camels, Altai Mountains, Mongolia

Let us not become weary in doing good, for at the proper time we will reap a harvest if we do not give up. Therefore, as we have opportunity, let us do good to all people.

—Galatians 6:9–10 NIV

📍 Stone lion sculptures, Forbidden City, Beijing, China

Turn away from evil and do good; seek peace and pursue it.

—Psalm 34:14 ESV

August 16

Mount Fuji and Lake Shoji, Japan

A friend loveth at all times, and a brother is born for adversity.

—Proverbs 17:17 KJV

August 17

Bastei Bridge, Saxon Switzerland National Park, Germany

And whenever you stand praying, forgive, if you have anything against anyone, so that your Father also who is in heaven may forgive you your trespasses.

—Mark 11:25 ESV

August 18

That [God] may give you the Spirit of wisdom and revelation, so that you may know him better. I pray that the eyes of your heart may be enlightened in order that you may know the hope to which he has called you, the riches of his glorious inheritance.

—Ephesians 1:17–18 NIV

African Elephant, Kruger National Park, South Africa

August 19

📍 Matryoshka dolls, Moscow, Russia

The LORD is nigh unto them that are of a broken heart; and saveth such as be of a contrite spirit.

—Psalm 34:18 KJV

August 20

Capitol Reef National Park, Utah, USA

A merry heart does good, like medicine, but a broken spirit dries the bones.

—Proverbs 17:22 NKJV

August 21

📍 Duomo di Milano, Milan, Italy

Render to Caesar the things that are Caesar's, and to God the things that are God's.

—Mark 12:17 ESV

August 22

📍 Black Sea coast, Yalta

We are God's handiwork, created in Christ Jesus to do good works, which God prepared in advance for us to do.

—Ephesians 2:10 NIV

August 23

📍 St. Peter's Church, Vienna, Austria

Many are the afflictions of the righteous, but the Lord delivers him out of them all.

—Psalm 34:19 ESV

August 24

📍 Jiulong waterfall, Yunnan, China

He who has knowledge spares his words. … Even a fool is counted wise when he holds his peace.

—Proverbs 17:27–28 NKJV

August 25

📍 Jefferson Memorial, Washington DC, USA

Be on guard, keep awake. For you do not know when the time will come.

—Mark 13:33 ESV

August 26

Sliema, Malta

I pray that out of his glorious riches he may strengthen you with power through his Spirit in your inner being, so that Christ may dwell in your hearts through faith.

—Ephesians 3:16, 17 NIV

August 27

Man at Work bronze sculpture, Bratislava, Slovakia

My soul shall be joyful in the LORD: it shall rejoice in his salvation.

—Psalm 35:9 KJV

August 28

📍 Table Mountain National Park, Cape Town, South Africa

The words of a man's mouth are as deep waters, and the wellspring of wisdom as a flowing brook.

—Proverbs 18:4 KJV

She has done what she could.

—Mark 14:8 ESV

August 29

Chain bridge, Budapest, Hungary

August 30

📍 Underwater cave, Raja Ampat islands, Indonesia

I pray that you … may … grasp how wide and long and high and deep is the love of Christ … that you may be filled to the measure of all the fullness of God.

—Ephesians 3:17–19 NIV

August 31

📍 The Martorana, Palermo, Sicily, Italy

Great is the LORD, who delights in the welfare of his servant!

—Psalm 35:27 ESV

September 1

Meteora, Greece

The name of the Lord is a strong tower; the righteous run to it and are safe.

—Proverbs 18:10 NKJV

September 2

📍 Gapstow bridge, Central Park, New York, USA

Watch and pray that you may not enter into temptation. The spirit indeed is willing, but the flesh is weak.

—Mark 14:38 ESV

September 3

Asian Mute Swan

To him who is able to do immeasurably more than all we ask or imagine, according to his power that is at work within us, to him be glory.

—Ephesians 3:20–21 NIV

September 4

Cupola of United States Capitol Building, Washington DC, USA

How excellent is thy lovingkindness, O God! Therefore the children of men put their trust under the shadow of thy wings.

—Psalm 36:7 KJV

September 5

El Capitan, Yosemite National Park, California, USA

The spirit of a man will sustain him in sickness, but who can bear a broken spirit?

—Proverbs 18:14 NKJV

September 6

📍 Bratislava castle, Slovakia

Go into all the world and proclaim the gospel to the whole creation. Whoever believes … will be saved.

—Mark 16:15–16 ESV

September 7

📍 Young Trumpeter Swans

Live a life worthy of the calling you have received.

—Ephesians 4:1 NIV

With thee is the fountain of life: in thy light shall we see light.

—Psalm 36:9 KJV

September 8

📍 Rua Augusta Arch, Lisbon, Portugal

September 9

📍 Ang Thong National Park, Koh Samui, Thailand

The heart of the prudent acquires knowledge, and the ear of the wise seeks knowledge.

—Proverbs 18:15 NKJV

September 10

Ocean Rock Restaurant, Zanzibar, Tanzania

I must preach the good news of the kingdom of God … for I was sent for this purpose.

—Luke 4:43 ESV

September 11

📍 Tanah Lot, Bali, Indonesia

Be … humble and gentle; be patient, bearing with one another in love.

—Ephesians 4:2 NIV

Cantonese opera puppets, Hong Kong, China

Delight yourself in the LORD, and he will give you the desires of your heart.

—Psalm 37:4 ESV

A man's gift makes room for him, and brings him before great men.

—Proverbs 18:16 NKJV

September 13

Kanarra Creek Slot Canyon, Zion National Park, Utah, USA

September 14

Potala Palace, Tibet, China

No one after drinking old wine desires new, for he says, "The old is good."

—Luke 5:39 ESV

September 15

📍 The Bosporus Strait, Istanbul, Turkey

In your anger do not sin: Do not let the sun go down while you are still angry.

—Ephesians 4:26 NIV

September 16

Healing of Blind Man of Jericho, by Leyden van Lucas van Leyden (1494 - 1533)

Commit your way to the LORD; trust in him, and he will act. He will bring forth your righteousness as the light, and your justice as the noonday.

—Psalm 37:5–6 ESV

September 17

Andaman Islands, Bay of Bengal, India

A brother offended is harder to win than a strong city, and contentions are like the bars of a castle.

—Proverbs 18:19 NKJV

September 18

United Church, Aylesbury, Saskatchewan, Canada

Be merciful, even as your Father is merciful.

—Luke 6:36 ESV

September 19

Get rid of all bitterness, rage and anger, brawling and slander, along with every form of malice. Be kind and compassionate to one another, forgiving each other, just as in Christ God forgave you.

—Ephesians 4:31–32 NIV

Golden Retriever puppies

September 20

"Kitchen" by David Teniers the Younger (1610 - 1690)

The meek shall inherit the earth; and shall delight themselves in the abundance of peace.

—Psalm 37:11 KJV

September 21

Haleakala volcano, Maui, Hawaii, U.S.A

A man who has friends must himself be friendly, but there is a friend who sticks closer than a brother.

—Proverbs 18:24 NKJV

September 22

Can a blind man lead a blind man? Will they not both fall into a pit?

—Luke 6:39 ESV

St. Marys Church of the Assumption, Bled Island, Julian Alps, Slovenia

September 23

📍 Common Blue Butterfly (Polyommatus icarus)

Live as children of light (for the fruit of the light consists in all goodness, righteousness and truth) and find out what pleases the Lord.

—Ephesians 5:8–10 NIV

📍 Detail from "The Last Judgement, Cathedral of Saint Mary of the Flower, Florence, Italy

The LORD knoweth the days of the upright: and their inheritance shall be for ever.

—Psalm 37:18 KJV

September 25

📍 Melissani Cave and Lake, Kefalonia Island, Greece

The discretion of a man makes him slow to anger, and his glory is to overlook a transgression.

—Proverbs 19:11 NKJV

September 26

📍 River Thames, London, England

A disciple is not above his teacher, but everyone when he is fully trained will be like his teacher.

—Luke 6:40 ESV

Be very careful …
how you live—not as
unwise but as wise,
making the most of
every opportunity,
because the days are
evil.

—Ephesians 5:15–16 NIV

September 27

Dubrovnik, Croatia

September 28

📍 Astronomical Clock Tower, Clusone, Lombardy, Italy

The steps of a good man are ordered by the LORD: and he delighteth in his way. Though he fall, he shall not be utterly cast down: for the LORD upholdeth him with his hand.

—Psalm 37:23–24 KJV

September 29

Lake Piva, Montenegro

He who has pity on the poor lends to the Lord, and He will pay back what he has given.

—Proverbs 19:17 NKJV

September 30

📍 Matsumoto castle, Nagano Prefecture, Japan

Each tree is known by its own fruit. … The good person … produces good, and the evil person … produces evil, for out of the abundance of the heart his mouth speaks.

—Luke 6:44–45 ESV

October 1

📍 Rice Paper Butterfly

Be strong in the Lord and in his mighty power.

—Ephesians 6:10 NIV

October 2

📍 Chicago Cultural Center, Chicago, USA

I have been young, and now am old, yet I have not seen the righteous forsaken or his children begging for bread.

—Psalm 37:25 ESV

October 3

Navagio Beach, Zakynthos Island, Greece

Counsel in the heart of man is like deep water, but a man of understanding will draw it out.

—Proverbs 20:5 NKJV

October 4

Do not weep.

—Luke 7:13 ESV

Orthodox Church, Odessa Oblast countryside, Ukraine

October 5

Durdle Door, Dorset, England

I thank my God every time I remember you. In all my prayers for all of you, I always pray with joy.

—Philippians 1:3–4 NIV

Basilica of Constantine, Trier, Germany

The salvation of the righteous is of the LORD: he is their strength in the time of trouble.

—Psalm 37:39 ESV

October 7

📍 Plitvice Lakes National Park, Croatia

Most men will proclaim each his own goodness, but who can find a faithful man?

—Proverbs 20:6 NKJV

October 8

📍 Fort Saint Nicolas, Medieval City of Rhodes, Greece

The blind receive their sight, the lame walk, lepers are cleansed, and the deaf hear, the dead are raised up, the poor have good news preached to them.

—Luke 7:22 ESV

This is my prayer: that your love may abound more and more … so that you may be able to discern what is best and may be … filled with the fruit of righteousness that comes through Jesus Christ.

—Philippians 1:9-11 NIV

October 9

Black jaguar, Wildlife Heritage Foundation, UK

October 10

The LORD … heard my cry. He drew me up from the pit of destruction, out of the miry bog, and set my feet upon a rock, making my steps secure. He put a new song in my mouth, a song of praise.

—Psalm 40:1–3 ESV

Mano del Desierto, Atacama Desert, Chile

October 11

Amargosa Range, Death Valley, California, USA

Every way of a man is right in his own eyes, but the Lord weighs the hearts.

—Proverbs 21:2 NKJV

October 12

Historic Villages of Shirakawago and Gokayama, White River Old-District, Japan

Wisdom is justified by all her children.

—Luke 7:35 ESV

October 13

Elk (Cervus canadensis), Grand Teton National Park, Wyoming, USA

Do nothing out of selfish ambition or vain conceit. Rather, in humility value others above yourselves, not looking to your own interests but each of you to the interests of the others.

—Philippians 2:3–4 NIV

October 14

📍 Statue of Emperor Qin Shi Huang, Xi'an, Shanxi, China

You have multiplied, O LORD my God, your wondrous deeds … none can compare with you! I will proclaim and tell of them, yet they are more than can be told.

—Psalm 40:5 ESV

October 15

Sugarloaf Mountain, Rio de Janeiro, Brazil

The plans of the diligent lead surely to plenty, but those of everyone who is hasty, surely to poverty.

—Proverbs 21:5 NKJV

October 16

Moscow State University, Moscow, Russia

Your faith has saved you; go in peace.

—Luke 7:50 ESV

October 17

Red Squirrel (Sciurus vulgaris)

It is God who works in you to will and to act in order to fulfill his good purpose.

—Philippians 2:13 NIV

October 18

Alcoves of the Provinces, Plaza de Espana, Seville, Spain

I delight to do your will, O my God; your law is within my heart.

—Psalm 40:8 ESV

October 19

Whoever guards his mouth and tongue keeps his soul from troubles.

—Proverbs 21:23 NKJV

Horseshoe Bend, Glen Canyon National Recreation Area, Arizona, USA

October 20

Hyangwonjeong Pavilion, Gyeongbokgung Palace grounds, Seoul, South Korea

Return to your home, and declare how much God has done for you.

—Luke 8:39 ESV

October 21

📍 Port of Hong Kong, Victoria Harbor, Hong Kong SAR, China

Forgetting what is behind and straining toward what is ahead, I press on toward the goal to win the prize for which God has called me.

—Philippians 3:13–14 NIV

October 22

📍 Millennium Monument, Heroes Square, Budapest, Hungary

May all who seek you rejoice and be glad in you; may those who love your salvation say continually, "Great is the LORD!"

—Psalm 40:16 ESV

October 23

Pentland Hills Regional Park, Scotland

A prudent man foresees evil and hides himself, but the simple pass on and are punished.

—Proverbs 22:3 NKJV

October 24

Vajdahunyad castle, Budapest, Hungary

Blessed … are those who hear the word of God and keep it!

—Luke 11:28 ESV

October 25

📍 Konitsa Bridge over Aoos River, Greece

Rejoice in the Lord always. I will say it again: Rejoice!

—Philippians 4:4 NIV

October 26

📍 Christ and the Apostles, Santa Maria de Montserrat Abbey, Catalonia, Spain

Blessed is the one who considers the poor! In the day of trouble the LORD delivers him.

—Psalm 41:1 ESV

By humility and the fear of the Lord are riches and honor and life.

—Proverbs 22:4 NKJV

October 27

Hang Mua Stairway, Ninh Binh, Vietnam

October 28

📍 Edinburgh Castle, Scotland

Your eye is the lamp of your body. When your eye is healthy, your whole body is full of light … as when a lamp with its rays gives you light.

—Luke 11:34,36 ESV

October 29

📍 Adelie Penguin, Antarctica

Let your gentleness be evident to all.

—Philippians 4:5 NIV

October 30

Tower Bridge and Girl with a Dolphin fountain, St Katharine Docks, London, England

As a deer pants for flowing streams, so pants my soul for you, O God. My soul thirsts for God, for the living God.

—Psalm 42:1–2 ESV

October 31

📍 Shiraito Falls, Fujinomiya, Japan

Train up a child in the way he should go: and when he is old, he will not depart from it.

—Proverbs 22:6 KJV

November 1

Are not five sparrows sold for two pennies? And not one of them is forgotten before God. Why, even the hairs of your head are all numbered. Fear not; you are of more value than many sparrows.

—Luke 12:6–7 ESV

Church of the Theotokos of the Sign, Dubrovitsy Estate, Moscow, Russia

November 2

Male Mandarin duck, Skalnaté Lake, Tatra National Park, Slovakia

Do not be anxious about anything, but in every situation, by prayer and petition, with thanksgiving, present your requests to God.

—Philippians 4:6 NIV

November 3

📍 St. Stephen's Basilica, Budapest, Hungary

Why are you cast down, O my soul, and why are you in turmoil within me? Hope in God.

—Psalm 42:11 ESV

November 4

Do you see a man who excels in his work? He will stand before kings.

—Proverbs 22:29 NKJV

Church of St. John the Baptist, Ribcev Laz, Triglav National Park, Slovenia

November 5

Puente Nuevo Bridge, Ronda, Andalusia, Spain

Be on your guard against all covetousness, for one's life does not consist in the abundance of his possessions.

—Luke 12:15 ESV

Whatever is true, whatever is noble, whatever is right, whatever is pure, whatever is lovely, whatever is admirable—if anything is excellent or praiseworthy—think about such things.

—Philippians 4:8 NIV

November 6

Arctic fox, Churchill, Manitoba, Canada

November 7

Prehistoric drawings, Magura Cave, Bulgaria

Send out your light and your truth; let them lead me.

—Psalm 43:3 ESV

November 8

📍 Source of the Rienz River, Tre Cime di Lavaredo, Tre Cime Nature Park, South Tyrol, Italy

Do not overwork to be rich. … For riches certainly make themselves wings.

—Proverbs 23:4–5 NKJV

November 9

📍 National Palace Museum, Taipei, Taiwan

Provide yourselves with … a treasure in the heavens that does not fail, where no thief approaches and no moth destroys. For where your treasure is, there will your heart be also.

—Luke 12:33–34 ESV

I have learned to be content whatever the circumstances. I know what it is to be in need, and I know what it is to have plenty. I have learned the secret of being content in any and every situation.

—Philippians 4:11–12 NIV

Transvaal lioness & cubs, Amakhala Game Reserve, Republic of South Africa

November 11

📍 The Raftman Statue, Torun, Poland

God is our refuge and strength, a very present help in trouble. Therefore we will not fear though the earth gives way, though the mountains be moved into the heart of the sea.

—Psalm 46:1–2 ESV

November 12

📍 Dolomites, South Tyrol, Italy

If you faint in the day of adversity, Your strength is small.

—Proverbs 24:10 NKJV

November 13

📍 Convent of the Order of Christ, Tomar, Portugal

One who is faithful in a very little is also faithful in much, and one who is dishonest in a very little is also dishonest in much.

—Luke 16:10 ESV

November 14

📍 Oriental white-eye in a wild Himalayan cherry tree, Koh Nangyuan, Thailand

Set your minds on things above, not on earthly things.

—Colossians 3:2 NIV

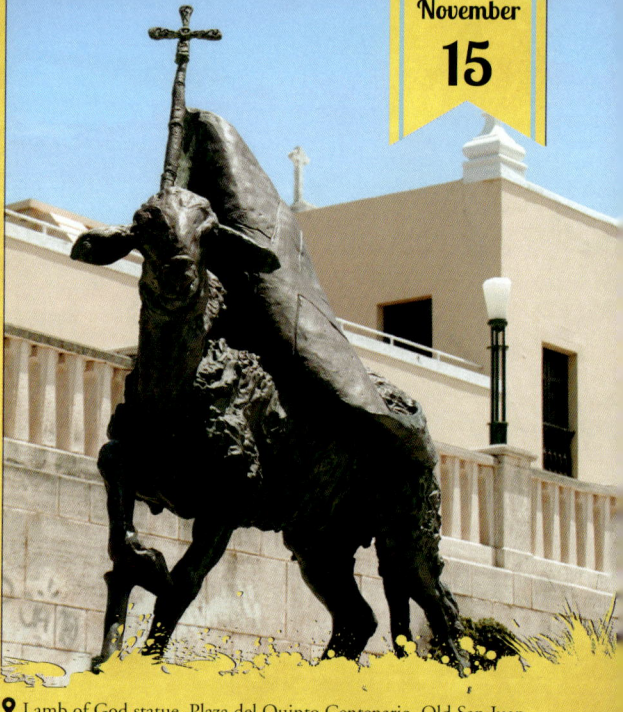

November 15

Call upon me in the day of trouble; I will deliver you, and you shall glorify me.

—Psalm 50:15 ESV

📍 Lamb of God statue, Plaza del Quinto Centenario, Old San Juan, Puerto Rico

November 16

📍 Haleakala, Maui, Hawaii, USA

Do not rejoice when your enemy falls, and do not let your heart be glad when he stumbles.

—Proverbs 24:17 NKJV

November 17

📍 Watchtower, Forbidden City, Beijing, China

The kingdom of God is not coming in ways that can be observed, nor will they say, "Look, here it is!" or "There!" … The kingdom of God is in … you.

—Luke 17:20–21 ESV

Clothe yourselves with compassion, kindness, humility, gentleness and patience. Bear with each other and forgive one another. … And over all these virtues put on love, which binds them all together.

—Colossians 3:12–14 NIV

November 18

📍 Eltz Castle, Wierschem, Germany

November 19

📍 Statue of King José I, Commerce Square, Lisbon, Portugal

Create in me a clean heart, O God, and renew a right spirit within me.

—Psalm 51:10 KJV

November 20

Do not stand in the place of the great; for it is better that he say to you, "Come up here," than that you should be put lower.

—Proverbs 25:6–7 NKJV

Mount Fuji, Japan

November 21

📍 Chengyangzhai Village, Sanjiang County, Guangxi, China

God so loved the world, that he gave his only Son, that whoever believes in him should not perish but have eternal life.

—John 3:16 ESV

November 22

We constantly pray for you, that our God may make you worthy of his calling, and that … he may bring to fruition your every desire for goodness and your every deed prompted by faith.

—2 Thessalonians 1:11 NIV

Dromedary, Arabian Desert, Dubai, United Arab Emirates

November 23

Lion Monument, Lucerne, Switzerland

Evening, and morning, and at noon, will I pray, and cry aloud: and he shall hear my voice.

—Psalm 55:17 KJV

📍 Earth Forest National Geopark, Zanda County, Xizang, China

A word fitly spoken is like apples of gold in settings of silver.

—Proverbs 25:11 NKJV

November 24

November 25

Ponte della Maddalena, Serchio River, Tuscany, Italy

Everyone who drinks of this water will be thirsty again, but whoever drinks of the water that I will give him will never be thirsty again.

—John 4:13 ESV

November 26

📍 Blue and Yellow Macaw (Ara ararauna) and Sugarloaf Mountain, Rio de Janeiro, Brazil

Godliness with contentment is great gain. For we brought nothing into the world, and we can take nothing out of it.

—1 Timothy 6:6–7 NIV

November 27

📍 Fountain of Justice, Römerberg, Frankfurt, Germany

Cast your burden on the LORD, and he will sustain you; he will never permit the righteous to be moved.

—Psalm 55:22 ESV

November 28

Mount Bromo, East Java, Indonesia

Have you found honey? Eat only as much as you need.

—Proverbs 25:16 NKJV

November 29

📍 Jioufen village, New Taipei City, Taiwan

God is spirit, and those who worship him must worship in spirit and truth.

—John 4:24 ESV

November 30

📍 Barn Owl (Tyto alba), Arizona, USA

The God of all grace … will himself restore you and make you strong, firm and steadfast.

—1 Peter 5:10 NIV

I will give thanks to you, O Lord. … Your steadfast love is great to the heavens, your faithfulness to the clouds. Be exalted, O God, above the heavens! Let your glory be over all the earth!

—Psalm 57:9–11 ESV

Park Güell, Carmel Hill, Barcelona, Spain

As cold waters to a thirsty soul, so is good news from a far country.

—Proverbs 25:25 KJV

December 2

Carpathian Mountains, Ukraine

December 3

📍 Giant Swing, Bangkok, Thailand

Do not judge by appearances, but judge with right judgment.

—John 7:24 ESV

December 4

Scarlet macaws, Corcovado National Park, Costa Rica

Pursue righteousness, godliness, faith, love, endurance and gentleness. Fight the good fight of the faith.

—1 Timothy 6:11–12 NIV

December 5

📍 Brandenburg Gate, Berlin, Germany

You have been to me a fortress and a refuge in the day of my distress. … I will sing praises to you, for you, O God, are my fortress, the God who shows me steadfast love.

—Psalm 59:16–17 ESV

December 6

📍 Mount Cook, Southern Alps, New Zealand

To seek one's own glory is not glory.

—Proverbs 25:27 NKJV

December 7

Let him who is without sin among you be the first to throw a stone.

—John 8:7 ESV

Santa Maria dell'Isola, Tropea, Calabria, Italy

December 8

If any of you lacks wisdom, you should ask God, who gives generously to all without finding fault, and it will be given to you.

—James 1:5 NIV

📍 Lilac-breasted roller, Kruger National Park, South Africa

Panorama of Parliament Square and Queen Elizabeth Tower in London, United Kingdom

With God we shall do valiantly.

—Psalm 60:12 ESV

Huay Mae Khamin Waterfalls, Sri Nakarin National Park, Thailand

Whoever has no rule over his own spirit is like a city broken down, without walls.

—Proverbs 25:28 NKJV

December 11

Gravensteen, Gent, Belgium

I am the light of the world. Whoever follows me will not walk in darkness, but will have the light of life.

—John 8:12 ESV

December 12

Lion cubs, Masai Mara, Kenya

Every good and perfect gift is from above, coming down from the Father ... who does not change like shifting shadows.

—James 1:17 NIV

Strahov Monastery library, Prague, Czech Republic

Hear my cry, O God. … When my heart is overwhelmed: lead me to the rock that is higher than I.

—Psalm 61:1–2 KJV

December 14

Banda Islands, Indonesia

Where there is no wood, the fire goes out; and where there is no talebearer, strife ceases. As charcoal is to burning coals, and wood to fire, so is a contentious man to kindle strife.

—Proverbs 26:20–21 NKJV

December 15

📍 Corfe Castle, Isle of Purbeck, Dorset, England

If you abide in my word, you are truly my disciples, and you will know the truth, and the truth will set you free.

—John 8:31–32 ESV

December 16

📍 Bald Eagles, Yellowstone National Park, Wyoming, USA

Who is wise and understanding among you? Let them show it by their good life, by deeds done in the humility that comes from wisdom.

—James 3:13 NIV

December 17

📍 Out of Order by David Mach, Kingston, London, England

If riches increase, set not your heart on them.

—Psalm 62:10 ESV

December 18

📍 Mendenhall Glacier, Juneau Borough, Alaska, USA

Do not boast about tomorrow, for you do not know what a day may bring forth.

—Proverbs 27:1 NKJV

Toledo, Spain

As I have loved you, you also are to love one another. By this all people will know that you are my disciples.

—John 13:34–35 ESV

December 20

📍 Weddell seal pup, Antarctica

The wisdom that comes from heaven is first of all pure; then peace-loving, considerate, submissive, full of mercy and good fruit, impartial and sincere.

—James 3:17 NIV

December 21

📍 Apollo Fountain, Palace of Versailles, Paris, France

My soul will be satisfied … and my mouth will praise you … when I remember you upon my bed, and meditate on you in the watches of the night.

—Psalm 63:5–6 ESV

December 22

📍 Caucasus Mountains, Georgia

Let another man praise you, and not your own mouth.

—Proverbs 27:2 NKJV

December 23

📍 Château de Chaumont, Chaumont-sur-Loire, Loir-et-Cher, France

You call me Teacher and Lord, and you are right. … If I then … have washed your feet, you also ought to wash one another's feet.

—John 13:13–14 ESV

December 24

📍 American Robin, Minnesota, USA

Come near to God and he will come near to you.

—James 4:8 NIV

December 25

📍 Christmas market, Frankfurt, Germany

By awesome deeds you answer us with righteousness, O God of our salvation, the hope of all the ends of the earth and of the farthest seas; the one who … established the mountains.

—Psalm 65:5–6 ESV

December 26

📍 Sol de Manana, Sur López Province, Bolivia

Faithful are the wounds of a friend, but the kisses of an enemy are deceitful.

—Proverbs 27:6 NKJV

December 27

If you know these things, blessed are you if you do them.

—John 13:17 ESV

Bran Castle, Bran, Romania

December 28

South African giraffe (Giraffa camelopardalis), Kruger National Park, South Africa

Humble yourselves before the Lord, and he will lift you up.

—James 4:10 NIV

December 29

📍 Portal of the Last Judgement, West façade, Notre Dame Cathedral, Paris, France

If I had cherished iniquity in my heart, the Lord would not have listened. But truly God has listened; he has attended to the voice of my prayer.

—Psalm 66:18, 19 ESV